A BRIEF HISTORY OF
UNDERPANTS

Timothy James Brown
BA (Hons, 3rd)

A BRIEF HISTORY OF
UNDERPANTS

Timothy James Brown
BA (Hons, 3rd)

Dedicated to my mother,
who once bought all my underpants
and who still would if I didn't stop her.

The author would like to thank the following for their enthusiastic supports:

Mark Rotenberg, Eric at Vintageskivvies.com, Ivy Leaf, Marcus Chown, Roz Mallard, Philippa Beazley, Lucian Randall, Sarah Macdonald, the long-suffering staff of the Compasses Inn, Tunbridge Wells, and of course the Mighty Noggin.

... and all those who requested anonymity. You know who you are.

Thanks are also due to Nicolas Cheetham and everyone at Quercus Books who now regret our phone call in the middle of the office Christmas party.

Written and illustrated by Tim Brown
Additional material by Giles Sparrow
Alpine underpants by Duncan Mallard
Cartoons by Mike Mosedale
Photography by Mark Harrison and Andrew Knight
Historic underpants by Tanya Featherstone
Embroidery by Hazel Muir

Design and editorial by Pikaia Imaging
Jacket by Two Associates

CONTENTS

FOREWORD

~

MY STRUGGLE WITH UNDERPANTS

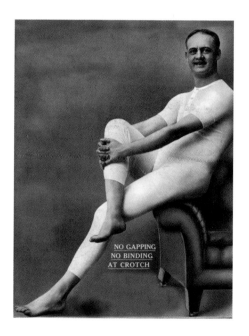

The author relaxes at home in a
Munsingwear union suit.

History is pants – you just don't know it yet. For some years now, I and a few like-minded colleagues have been engaged in a long and bitter struggle to reveal the truth. At first we worked underground, through a network of post-office boxes, anonymous email accounts and drop points at telephone kiosks, charity shops and gentlemen's lavatories across the home counties. But increasingly we have dared to speak the truth that one could previously only whisper: throughout most of the 20th century, academic historians have been engaged in a systematic coverup of the crucial role of undertrouserage and its associated fittings in world history.

Now, at last, the truth can be revealed. Welcome, dear reader, to the first accurate, deeply researched and probing investigation of the epic history of the underpant. It has taken me many years, cast adrift in the wilderness; rejected by many, pursued by others, to find a publisher courageous enough to put my work into print. Needless to say, some still find the very mention of underpants tasteless or provocative, and no doubt there are many respected academics and historians who will appear to dismiss my historical observations as inaccurate, puerile or just plain wrong. I am ready to deal with such backward 'pantist' thinking from these people – the kind of so-called academics who think it's acceptable never to return my emails, never to invite me on nights out with other historians, and who recently had an ASBO placed on me for causing a disturbance in the Reading Room of the British Library.

To the many people who have supported me, I give thanks. We have together walked a lonely road to a full understanding of underwear. Without such people as Mr W of Dagenham, Errol Mohican of Bear Seed Rapids, Wichita, and the man who leaves things in bags by my front door, this book could never have been possible. Above all, I would like to pay homage to my dear departed Uncle Minty who, as I stand here today with my pants held high, would, I am sure, be noticeably proud.

Timothy James Brown BA (Hons, 3rd)
The Pantiles, Tunbridge Wells
2008

INTRODUCTION

~

THE QUEST FOR PANTS

Underpants, underwear, call them what you will, they are the most elusive of things in history, and we glimpse them as if in a dream. According to my well-thumbed dictionary, the very name is a chimera of the Germanic word *unter*, meaning 'beneath', and the ancient Greek *phantasioo*, meaning 'cause to imagine'. How appropriate, given that what little we know about the history of our most intimate of garments we can only glimpse through a crack in the known records.

Underpants do not fossilise, and in all but a few cases they decay rapidly after burial, whether it be through disposal on the local midden or interment in the most reverent circumstances. As a result, it is a fortunate archaeologist that stumbles upon a preserved unmentionable.

For the dedicated pantologist, the hunt for the truth represents a voyage of discovery more fantastic than any adventure by Lara Croft, Indiana Jones or Kate Humble. The struggle is made all the more difficult by the fact that, since the Middle Ages, underwear has been a source of embarrassment and childish humour. It is only in recent years that it has become a suitable subject for discussion in polite society, let alone academic research.

And yet pants are pivotal: in a nutshell, and as many of our most respected television newscasters can attest, comfortable underwear can be liberating, invigorating and a source of pride. If uncomfortable, these very same garments can transform the wearer into a meek, submissive slave, ready to follow anyone who can offer the merest hint of loin-based support. Powerful men long ago learned how to suppress the masses with inhuman smalls, debilitating corsets and the sinister sock suspender.

Quite simply, I feel the quest for the true story of underpants is a quest for the story of humanity itself. It is a saga of pain and suffering, of agony and ecstasy, of rinsing and repeating; the fantastic tale of a brave few who have risen above the rest, placing themselves at huge risk of embarrassment, injury and social rejection in order to advance the technology and understanding of underwear.

However, it should be noted that this book runs to a mere 128 pages, and so is a pale shadow of the monumental 15-volume work with which I first approached my publisher, surprising him one morning as he left the Groucho Club after a particularly long lunch.

This smaller 'pocket' format severely restricts the scope of the work. There is no room, for example, for the Boxer Rebellion, in which a small European force was besieged in Peking for 55 days by opium-crazed Chinese laundrymen incensed by persistent stains.

Likewise I note that my controversial conclusions on Native American bisonwear, Basque Separatism, the Balkan Underpant Wars and the sad tale of Vlad the Embroiderer have been eviscerated by a junior editor with no sense of their true historical import.

Emily Kronkite, a personal heroine of mine and the first anchorwoman to mention underwear live on U.S.

And political correctness and the needs of the 'international market' apparently preclude mention of recent political issues such as the renaming of the French Knicker as the Freedom Knicker in five U.S. states. As always, the world of the underpant is never far from controversy

television. She is seen here prior to her controversial dismissal for pressing Nixon over his use of Cuban string vests.

and if this work, however small and garishly bound it might be, goes some way to opening minds, then I will have achieved something.

Before we begin, however, I wish to make my position clear on the thorny issue of underpants and lewd activities. For the record, I should state that, as an avowed Paxmanist, I consider the connection so many have made between underpants and baby-making to be of secondary importance to their main functions of support, absorbency and confidence building. While I cannot entirely ignore the fact that many use underpants as a means of sexual attraction, for me sex is not a big thing, and in the course of this work it has become even smaller, as my housekeeper will readily attest. Those who are obsessed with such associations are a blight on my studies and have ruined many of my lectures by reacting in a trivial manner to the slightest mention of words such as 'probe', 'loin' and 'strap'. I hope that my present readers will accept this work in the spirit in which it is intended.

The most mysterious of the La Purla murals may have functioned as a primitive pattern-book. The underpant symbolism is clear. Less obvious is the sock-like motif at lower right.

IN THE BEGINNING

THE YEAR DOT

What makes humanity unique, and what raises our species above the animals? Some have argued that it is our large brains, others that it is our ability to use tools. But controversial new evidence, including bone fly-buttons from Ethiopia's Olduvai Gorge, the famous buckskin tanga from the La Purla tar pits, and the fabulous cave paintings of *La Grotte de Corsetière*, seems to clinch the matter: pants have been man's steadfast companions since the dawn of consciousness.

A few brave anthropologists have even speculated that it was the introduction of groinal support which finally allowed our ancestors to walk upright, freeing their hands for gripping tools, and allowing their heads to swell to abnormal size. If this was indeed the case, then the invention of the pant may have been directly responsible for the arrival of *Homo erectus*.

Textbook representations of the 'ascent of man' frequently fail to acknowledge the importance of underpants in the evolutionary story. This version sets the record straight – although there is increasing evidence that early man didn't know quite what to do with his new invention.

PANTS OF DAWN

ONE MILLION YEARS B.C.

The arrival of the Ice Age was a major setback for prehistoric man, but our ancestors rose to the challenge with new, improved underwear based on so-called 'smart' materials such as sabre-toothed tigerskin (ideally with the sabre-toothed tiger removed) and mammoth scrotum. Around one million years B.C., the mysterious Eve-like figure that palaeopantologists know simply as 'Dawn of Civilisation' invented the fur bikini, establishing a fashion that would last right up until people started wearing bedsheets.

At about the same time, the fossil record indicates that early man also investigated the groin-insulating properties of live animals, the most versatile of which proved to be *Choloepus didactylus*, the two-toed sloth. However, these short-lived experiments ended in disaster for both parties, and some evolutionary biologists believe that this may explain the present-day sloth's shy, arboreal lifestyle.

Raquel Welch (in the role of Dawn) and an unnamed friend model the hottest fashions for spring one million B.C., shortly before making their escape from a giant lizard with unconvincingly glued-on horns.

A classical rendition of the Eden story captures the moment when Eve shows Adam her apples for the first time. Despite the Bible's insistence that Adam had nothing to be ashamed of, his strategic placement of convenient ground cover suggests otherwise.

OUT OF EDEN

10.30 A.M., 4004 B.C.

A distant memory of the early importance of pants survives in the Book of Genesis, possibly the world's greatest underwear-related creation myth. According to this account, the first primitive his-and-hers thongs were invented in November 4004 B.C., after Eve, troubled in her sleep by visits from a persistent snake, insisted that Adam cover himself up in future – just as soon as they had finished those delicious apples over there...

This charming story may be the origin of the phrase 'winter drawers on', but sadly when the infuriated head gardener returned, he took little interest in their new clothing innovations, and instead had them chased out of the Garden of Eden and barred as a public nuisance. As a result, we know distressingly little about the operating principles of the self-supporting fig leaf.

CRADLES OF CIVILISATION

3000 B.C.

The developing story of underwear becomes much easier to trace with the arrival of the first written records. Early cuneiform washing instructions have been found at famous Middle Eastern sites including Ur, Nippur and Um-urr, and of course the name Mesopotamia itself translates loosely as 'land between two bottoms'.

Nevertheless, the continued use of roughly sewn animal skins, often with the hooves still attached, meant the Babylonians, Chaldeans and Assyrians suffered severe chafing and lack of support in the vital gusset region. The invention of moisturiser by the Ninevites offered some relief, but it was not until the famous Tiglath-Pileser IV introduced woven cloth and, with it, the first simple trunks, that Mesopotamian civilisation could truly flourish.

A famous sketch by Leonard Woolley from the so-called 'Great Laundry Basket of Ur', where King Utnapishtim was buried alongside 200 pairs of sacrificial underpants. Agatha Christie was a frequent visitor to the dig – her struggles to find comfortable underwear in the parched climate are thought to have inspired the title of Murder in Mesopotamia.

PANTS ON THE NILE

2500–1000 B.C.

Meanwhile, another great civilisation was flowering along the banks of the Nile. Famous for their monumental erections, such as the Sphinx and the Pyramids, the Egyptians were great engineers, and found their own solution to the long-running support problem through the development of the pre-formed papyrus thong with aloe vera padding – a vital comfort for people who apparently spent most of their lives walking sideways and hauling sandstone blocks around the desert.

Freed from such practical considerations, the bling-fixated pharaohs developed ornate, solid gold G-strings for ceremonial wear, and were frequently buried with thousands of pairs of miniature *pianti* for use in the next world. Since the afterlife was reserved for those who died without a stain on their character, Egyptians believed that, at the moment of death, their underpants would be inspected by the ibis-headed god Thoth. As a result, later dynasties became obsessed with the quest for an efficient fabric whitener.

A selection of Egyptian underwear myths recorded on a papyrus from the Tomb of Ne-ther-titi II. Top left: handmaidens of Isis pray for the coming of the Great Blue-Whitener. Top right: the three sons of Sesostris – inventors of the high-waisted long john, the mankini and the ankh-front. Lower left: Menkhare ponders the failure of his lucky pants when introduced to Princess Jadagudi of Punt. Lower right: the heretic pharaoh Akhenaten wrestles the mythical trouser-snake (note the eccentric god-king's crocodile shoes and beetle haircut).

19

Thrusting young philosophers Pantocrates and Thongynides the Elder hanging out at the Acropolis prior to a traditional Athenian symposium on the prominent issue of smalls. Note that, while the Greeks clearly appreciated the importance of clothes, they had no sense of priority about where they should be worn.

A GREEK TRAGEDY

500 B.C.

The ancient Greeks had many admirable features, and they laid the bedrock for much of Western Civilisation, but when it came to the crucial issue of underwear, they proved sadly lacking – often quite literally. Archaeological evidence points to a dispiriting lack of underfoundations in the academies of Athens – a trend that began in the hero-worship of naked athletes at the Olympic Games. It was made widely acceptable by Archimedes' celebratory streak through the streets of Syracuse (following his discovery of Archimedes' Screw, predecessor of the modern spin drier).

From this point on, the Greeks became incorrigible nudists, so it's little wonder Alexander the Great turned out the way he did. Quite apart from the lack of physical support, an all-nude lifestyle caused a lot of social problems for the ancient Greeks, who found they had to stop their usual vigorous social intercourse and conceal themselves behind any convenient object whenever a sculptor came past.

Considering their persistent want of coverage in the mid-hip area, it's little wonder the Greeks eventually came up with a deity who came pre-briefed. This sculpture shows the mischievous Pan toying with his flute in a classical grove.

21

GO TELL THE SPARTANS

480 B.C.

Even as the Athenians were foolishly abandoning their pants, their near neighbours the Spartans were taking athletic support to a new level. Shortly after devising a loincloth made from a single square of cleverly folded chamois leather, the Spartan general Leonidas received word of a mighty army of oiled-up Persians aiming to penetrate the pass at Thermalopylae, well known as Greece's back entrance.

While the Athenians sat around philosophising, Leonidas, famed as an expert on rearguard actions, engaged the Persians at the pass, aided only by 300 muscular friends (and 1,300 slaves that the history books tend to ignore). The heroic Spartan defence slowed the Persian advance for several days, buying time for the Greek navy to prepare its sailors for the Battle of Salamis, a sausage competition that saw the Persians decisively beaten off.

A fully armed Spartan warrior presented a formidable package, and was not the sort of person you wanted to run into down a darkened passage.

Chisel-jawed rebel Spartacus led a slave revolt in protest against the imposition of the new Agrippan Grasper. Modern scholars believe he also had a personal grudge against his master, influential Roman performance artist Damianus Hirstus.

THE GLORY
THAT WAS ROME

300 B.C.–400 A.D.

Abandoning the decadence of the pant-shunning Greeks, the Roman Republic heralded a golden age built on a belief in robust, durable undertrouserage. With these strong foundations, Rome was soon able to extend its reach across the Mediterranean world and beyond, bringing the benefits of the *Pants Romana* even as far as our backward little island.

Metalled roads and the introduction of the double-ply padded gusset allowed a typical legion to easily outmanoeuvre barbarian enemies who had barely mastered the most basic trunk technology. For all this, Rome had a dark side, manifested in Agrippa's development of brutal slave undergarments that restricted personal freedom in more ways than one.

Mercury, famed for his racy behaviour and alabaster white smalls.

Hello tiger: a scene from Mel Gibson's forthcoming epic Daniel in the Lion's Den, *starring the cast of* Friends.

BIBLICAL SMALLS

0

The record of underwear in the Bible is scanty – accounts of Pontius Pilate's Triumph are probably a translation error on the part of King James, while Salome's Dance of the Seven Veils is sadly lacking in detail. However, a few gems do shine through – Saint Paul's work as a tax inspector on the road to Damascus, for instance, which must have brought him into regular contact with the cloth-merchants of that fine city (whose trunks were famed across the ancient world, even as far as the parts of Libya around Cyrene).

Old Testament hero Daniel is thought to have fallen head first into the lion's den during a futile search for a leopardskin tanga, and the curious historian is left pondering exactly what King David used for a slingshot.

Biblical minx Salome pioneered many innovations, including table dancing and complex menu alterations. For the pantologist there is the tantalising hint that she may also have pioneered the first fully organic girdle, as seen in this publicity shot for Sir Kenneth Rustle's 1923 production of Salome's Last Dance at the Windmill Theatre.

Ben Her displays her virginiform brassiere to the crowds in a pivotal scene from Tobias Meyer's classic film of her life, Hot Times at the Hippodrome *(1972).*

BEN HER

64 A.D.

Among the most famous of all Roman gladiators was the female charioteer Judith Ben Her, a princess of the British Iceni tribe (whose previous queen, Boudicca, had also made something of a name for herself on the chariot circuit). Intrigued by tales of the Roman Triumph, the young Judith attempted to break into the Governor's palace and make off with his wife's trousseau, but was captured and shipped off to Rome where the Emperor Nero decided to make an example of her.

However, Nero's fearsome wife Poppaea found out and insisted that she instead be forced to compete for her life in Rome's barbaric games. At the Hippodrome, Judith's outstanding talent put her in front and she won by a head, a neck and a bust. Completing a lap of honour, she threw her lucky armour to the crowd, then made her escape, trailing sparks that set much of the city alight. Nero must have been a spectator to Judith's topless rampage. Indeed, he may have felt it deserved a musical accompaniment, perhaps one reason why he was fiddling while Rome burned.

PANTS OF THE VANDALS

450 A.D.

Empires are like underpants – they go down as well as up. And so it was with Rome. As the heart of the empire lapsed into decadence and shirked its duty as purveyor of stout, reliable briefs, the armies of Huns, Vandals and Goths took a violent dislike to what they saw as increasingy deviant Roman underwear.

The image of Rome's invincible might was irretrievably damaged when a scouting party of Ostrogoths ambushed the Legio II Augusta in the middle of a platoon production of *Caligula's Aunt*, capturing the centurion Quintus Crispus in full drag. Henceforth the advancing tribes swept across the collapsing Empire, enforcing a back-to-basics regime of traditional animal-skin or hessian kecks that culminated in the famously barbaric 'Sack of Rome'.

King Alaric of the Visigoths models the latest in cross-cut barbarian underwear in a contemporary illustration. The fearsome nature of the inflated Visigoth 'headpant' and their habit of using it as a weapon in close-quarters combat is thought to be responsible for the phrase 'getting the horn'.

Dominatia, Queen of the Goths, leads the charge at the Battle of the Reeperbahn.

31

Yey, at first those Pictish menne saith unto him they need not the LORD's underthings, for they wert "rocke-harde" and might endure even the fiercest winter "in the nip, like, as long as I got me tabs". And the Blessed Michael pondered these things, and he called upon the LORD to send his most merciful hailstorm, the like of which the land hath not seen thereuntofore. And there was greate perturbation throughout the land, and three-score thousand died of thee haile or thee exposure or thee feare, in the LORD's mercy. And after three days, the King of the Geordiemenne did come again unto the Saint, and saith unto him "These kecks, like – how much was yaa sayin?" And from that moment on, the people of Geordieland wore most rightfully the undergarments of the LORD, and the Blessed St Michael knew he had indeed doneth the right thinge.

THE DARK AGES

500–800 A.D.

Nowhere was the collapse of Roman support felt more keenly than in the outlying province of Britannia, where the civilised citizens found themselves abruptly overrun from all sides. Invaders included the Picts from Scotland, the Scots from Ireland, and the Irish, presumably from Pictland. Jutes and Angles also piled in, led by the fearsome Hengist and his horse. Before long, most of Britain was back to wode body paint, hessian trunks and simple corsets made from brambles.

Fortunately, in 600 A.D., Pope Benedict the Sensitive dispatched a team of crack missionaries from Rome to reintroduce Christianity, civilisation and godly underwear to the rest of Europe. At first, these saintly men received a hostile welcome, but through their steadfast dedication and the obvious benefits of a supportive gusset with tailored waistband, Christianity largely prevailed, except on Friday and Saturday nights when pagan madness was still the norm. This is a trend that can still be seen when visiting Reading town centre on a bank holiday weekend.

Saint Michael brings underpants to the Geordies:
a medieval illumination from the Life of Saint Michael
shows the noble saint received by tribesmen somewhere
near Gateshead.

The Saga of Eric the Red Raw *tells of an epic journey into the unknown. Eric is reputed to have never sat down during the arduous journey from Greenland to Vinland, and to have glowed for several hours after sunset.*

VIKINGS GO BERSERK

900 A.D.

For the average European, the well-built Scandinavian warriors known as Vikings were a force to be reckoned with, leading a campaign of rape, loot and pillage that struck particular fear into the hearts of local sailors, farmyard animals and monks. And while many of them were indeed somewhat berserk, it's little wonder when one considers the pressure they were under.

Recent research has discovered that the Viking ships had sails made entirely of the *underbøckser* or Norse Longpant, sewn together for the length of the journey and only separated and distributed among the crew when the ship reached land. Tough though these warriors were, prolonged exposure to Arctic winds and splintered seats took its toll on the Viking behind, and as their voyages of self-exploration reached as far as Greenland and the New World, one can only guess at how abrasive shipboard relations might get. The famous explorer Eric the Red Raw is reputed to have discovered Newfoundland, Vinland and Disneyland during his fruitless quest for a natural source of Neutrogena.

PRO hOMO VIRILE MODERNE

THE DOMESDAY PANT

1066

Chain mail was all the rage by the end of the Dark Ages. Smart, practical and capable of sustaining an archery attack, a set of armoured underwear was ideal for the modern man who was prepared to overlook the side issue of rust for the sake of a relatively quiet life. At the centre of this burgeoning trade were the massive mail-order warehouses of Basingstoke, who sent their embroidered catalogues all over Christendom.

Unfortunately, courier services at the time were virtually non-existent. Any deliveries had to brave pirates, storms and regular postal strikes before they eventually arrived – and even then they were often the wrong size or colour. One of Basingstoke's biggest customers, William, Duke of Normandy, finally snapped in 1066 after receiving a 'Sorry you were out' card while occupying Caen with 10,000 fully armed troops and their camp followers. Already well known as a short-tempered French bastard, William was determined to have it out with customer services, and immediately set sail for England, slaughtering any sales representatives he could lay his hands on before ordering a complete census of Saxon underwear just to be difficult.

Celebrities in their own right, Sir Gavin the Proud and Percy Small model the final spring range of the 1066 menswear catalogue. Caught by William trying to escape to Norway, Small and Proud were sentenced to death by mangle.

UNCOMFORTABLE KNIGHTS

1100

In 1095, Pope Urban II declared the crusading season officially open and the bloodthirsty nobility of Europe, tired of oppressing the peasantry, decamped en masse to go and oppress the Holy Land instead. However, things began to go badly wrong shortly after the fall of Jerusalem, as the crusaders discovered that their heavy armour and chain mail undervests were ill-suited to the Middle Eastern climate.

Soon the knights were in a terrible state, and took to hanging around in just their damask trunk-and-singlet combinations. In the circumstances, it's little wonder the Saracens, equipped with better-designed and looser fitting underlayers firmly attached with Arab straps, swiftly beat off the crusaders. Soon, their only stronghold was, appropriately enough, the port city of Acre. Even Richard the Lionheart's attempts to retake Jerusalem succumbed to plague, heat and an outbreak of chafing – though the noble general Saladin is said to have shown both admiration and compassion for his rival by sending him a pot of aloe vera gel.

Richard the Lionheart (left) snapped in an intimate moment relaxing with his special friend Christopher. Camp followers were an integral part of a well-organised crusade – note Christopher's unusual weapon.

THE AGE OF CHIVALRY

1300

After his resounding defeat in the Crusades, Queen Eleanor of Westphalia, like many noblewomen, was understandably horror-struck at the idea of her husband returning home, flinging off his armour and demanding hourly applications of linament to his inner groin. And so, desperate to forestall King Udo the Intractable's testosterone-charged attentions, she came up with possibly the greatest confidence trick of all time.

Hiring a team of itinerant poets to knock out some heroic epics about 'courtly love', she successfully convinced her husband (and the entire knightly caste of northwestern Europe) to keep their uncomfortable armoured leggings on for a couple more centuries, and carry on slashing each other to bits in ritual combat. In return, they hoped to win a favour from a pretty girl, though on most occasions this turned out to be just a handkerchief. It says something about the returning crusaders' state of mind that they fell for this, although some did attempt to take revenge with the invention of the chastity belt.

The Duchess Estelle de Poitou 'gets them out for the lords' in one of the less challenging scenes from the notorious Lady and the Unicorn tapestry, a triumph of French 'specialist' embroidery.

*In a pivotal scene from 'Circle 3a', Dante and Virgil watch in horror as
Count Gandolfo Scarlioni and the Bishop of Utrecht have their breaches loosened prior
to torture at the hands of the demons Auld Pantywaiste, Schrimblefetzer, and
Jack O'the Codling.*

DANTE'S IN THERMALS

1321

No one summed up the medieval world view, and the pivotal position of pants in the average Middle-Aged mind, like Italian poet Dante Alighieri. What his *Divine Comedy* lacks in jokes, it makes up for in rude bits, knowing winks to his target audience of inbred Italian nobility and constant references to God. Throughout the work, Dante is led on an allegorical journey through hell, purgatory and heaven by the spirit of the Roman poet Virgil*.

Perhaps metaphorically, few readers make it to paradise because all the good stuff is in hell – and this includes the material of most interest to bibliopantologists. A recently discovered manuscript copy of the *Inferno* reveals Dante had planned to insert an additional circle of hell ('Circle 3a') in which those who had failed to keep their underpants clean were punished by an assortment of nightmarish demons armed with outlandish codpieces.

---

* *These days, of course, Virgil is chiefly remembered for the epic schoolboy-torturing poem, The Aeneid, which ironically provided a protective layer in the rear of a fair few pairs of pants, back in the days when Latin and corporal punishment formed the twin pillars of our nation's schools.*

THE MARTYRDOM OF ANNE SOMMERS

1420

Born of noble blood, Lady Anne Sommers founded her own order of nuns, The Sisterhood of the Red Hot Mamas, in the early 15th century, opening her first convent in what is now London's Soho district. Identifying an untapped public demand, the nuns spent much of their time developing unusual habits from such exotic materials as rubber, otter pelts and hemp.

This soon drew the annoyance of Rome, and the sinister Monsignor La Sensa was duly dispatched to tie down the wayward sisters. Forced to denounce plunging necklines and all things saucy, Sommers was tortured with a French Tickler for five days before finally confessing to shopping with the devil. Burnt at the stake, she later appeared to the Bishop of Mayfair in a series of fevered dreams, alongside a goat and a group of enthusiastic young acrobats from Liège.

Composed to the last, Anne Sommers faces death with
a saucy wink and fabulous legs. Doubtless it would
warm her heart to know that the site of her sacrifice
still plays host to a weekly celebration of fetishwear.

After nine weeks at sea, Columbus comes ashore at Hispaniola.
While laundry was clearly the first priority for his crewmen, their captain barters
in the foreground for exotic native underpinnings.

A NEW WORLD

1492

By the late 15th century, the increasingly elaborate underwear stylings of Catholic Europe were putting unprecedented strain on the always-stretched silk supply. Determined to turn this to their advantage, Queen Isabella of Castile and King Ferdinand of Aragon decided to sponsor enterprising sailor Christopher Columbus's plan to cut the Silk Road out of things altogether, and find a direct route to the legendary lingerie workshops of the Far East.

As we all know, things didn't work out quite this way, and Ferdinand and Isabella had to abandon their plans for a range of 'C&A' branded underwear. The various tribes of the Americas weren't too happy at being discovered either, as the arrival of rapacious conquistadors in search of gold, underwear and gold underwear put an end to their tranquil life of chocolate, tobacco and mass human sacrifice.

Performing a star-jump to express his delight at finally aquiring decent underwear, Ronaldo Vitruvius proudly models what was soon known at the 'why oh why oh why front'. Previously, the eight-limbed star player and top goal scorer of ACF Fiorentina had been forced to glue felt to himself in order to maintain his modesty.

RENAISSANCE MAN

1509

During idle moments between inventing helicopters, the Corby Trouser Press and the Pot Noodle, the great Leonardo da Vinci often busied himself with the development of post-medieval smalls. His first brush with underpants came at the siege of Padua in 1509, when he suggested catapulting the gravy-stained trunks of the army cook over the city walls in order to force a surrender. This had the desired effect, although the attackers were then so reluctant to enter the town that it lay deserted for five weeks.

However, Leonardo's greatest triumph came when he was commissioned by Ronaldo Vitruvius, the famous eight-limbed Florentine sportsman and womaniser, to create a pant suitable for his unique body. The resulting four-legged wonderbrief still ranks among the most complex underwear ever made, and its exact construction remains a matter of much debate amongst scholars.

Take them down! Cardinal La Sensa and his fearsome acolyte Sister Wendy live up to their lurid reputation in a still from Hammer's 1964 reimagining of the Inquisition, Terror at Castle Unterhosen.

LA SENSA STRIKES BACK

1518

In 1517, Martin Luther brought years of discontented rumblings over self-indulgent priests to a head by decisively hammering his standard-issue clerical support to the door of Wittenberg Cathedral. This was the start of the Reformation, and soon everyone was joining in.

Johannes Gutenberg printed the first widely distributed manual of underwear design on a converted mangle, and the ascetic Swiss John Calvin roamed the land as an itinerant preacher, clad only in the roughly sewn burlap jockstrap that became known to the local German-speaking populace as 'Calvin's Kleines'. Desperate to reinforce their authority, the Catholic Church launched a Counter-Reformation, unleashing the Inquisition, led by the latest offspring of the fearsome La Sensa dynasty.

Princess Betty of Schleswig-Holstein comes face-to-spike with the full horror of La Sensa's Inquisition following an ill-judged remark about the Bishop of Hamburg's visible panty line.

Taking a break from heated negotiations in the sweltering French summer, Henry impresses the local womenfolk by parading his hot dog, while Francis flaunts a substantial broadsword.

FIELD OF THE LOINCLOTHS OF GOLD

1520

With the coronation of Henry VIII, England got its first fashion-conscious monarch. No longer would royalty be content to slum it in the same kecks as the proles – from now on, only the finest imported silks and damasks would be deemed fit to cosset the royal nethers. As a result, Henry's ever-expanding waistline put an unprecedented strain on both his corsets and the Exchequer.

Things wouldn't have been so bad if an equally conspicuous consumer hadn't simultaneously sat on the French throne. When Henry met the infamous *Roi de Bling*, Francis I, for treaty discussions in a field near Calais, the one-upmanship got entirely out of hand. Having encrusted everything else with as much precious metal as they could lay their hands on, the two monarchs finally reached a deal after stripping to their gold lamé boxers.

Recently discovered candid snaps of Henry's six wives. Left to right: Katherine the Arrogant, Anne of Cleavage, Doctor Quinn Medicine Woman, Anne of No Cleavage, Katharine Hepburn, Audrey Hepburn.

THE AGE OF EXPLORERS

1521

The discovery of the Americas was merely one highlight in a century or more of global exploration, during which European merchants travelled far and wide. As one might expect, underclothes were pivotal to the new trading empires in more ways than one. Belgian designer Gerardus Damarticus devised the first clinker-built hosiery capable of withstanding months of tossing in a rough sea, and the attendant saturation with salty fluid.

Inspired by this, Portuguese navigator Ferdinand Magellan set sail with his fleet on a mission to circumnavigate the world, with a crew of 20 and just three pairs of pants between them. The voyage met with mixed fortunes – Magellan himself ended up in dire straits, but most of his crew survived after improvising simple jockstraps from their vessels' mizzen sails.

An exotic high priestess of the South Sea Islands performs a charming traditional dance shortly before eviscerating a sacrificial victim with her protruberances.

One size fits all: long, damp sea voyages often left travellers with feverish dreams of strange and exotic creatures, taunting them with the promise of comfortable underwear.

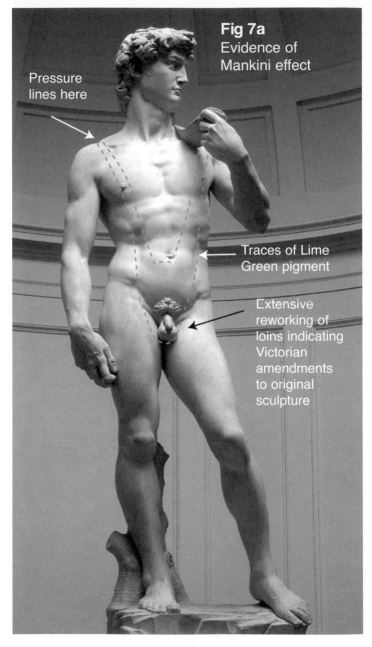

Fig 7a
Evidence of
Mankini effect

Pressure
lines here

Traces of Lime
Green pigment

Extensive
reworking of
loins indicating
Victorian
amendments
to original
sculpture

THE MICHELANGELO CODPIECE

1530

Why did the great Italian artist Michelangelo spend so much time sculpting and painting muscular young men? New research seems to reveal a truth more lurid than any airport thriller. Painstaking analysis of Michelangelo's works by Professor Hung Warren of the University of Daytona Beach shows that many have been 'touched up', presumably after the artist's death.

Warren's reconstructions, reproduced here with permission, show the secret pantosymbology present in the originals. The statue of David, long held as an ideal of male beauty, shows clear signs of having had work done around the inner thigh, while X-rays reveal a ghostly outline passing between the hands of God and Man. Could Michelangelo have been a member of the Panticrucians, a secretive sect handing down lost knowledge of ancient underwear design? Or was there some other reason, that we can barely guess at, for his interest in the male form?

Fig 15

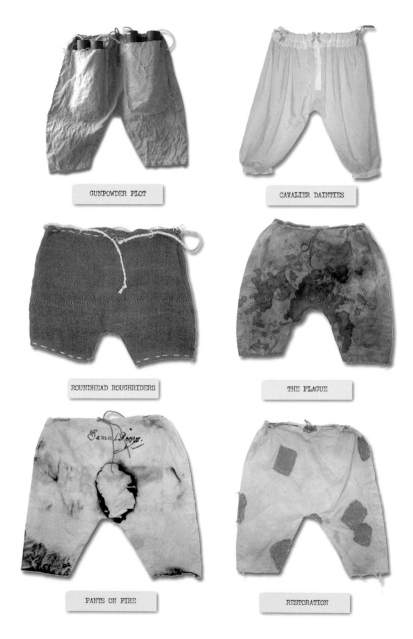

GUNPOWDER PLOT

CAVALIER DAINTIES

ROUNDHEAD ROUGHRIDERS

THE PLAGUE

PANTS ON FIRE

RESTORATION

A CENTURY OF WOES

1600–1700

The 1600s were a pivotal period in the history of underwear, as the rare display of period trunks preserved in the Featherstone Collection (reproduced left) reveals. Throughout the century, the repercussions of the Reformation rumbled on. Guido Fawkes and his fellow conspirators used specially customised Italian *pantaloni* in their vain attempt to stop Parliament imposing punitive taxes on Catholic silk. The rise of Puritanism spawned numerous splinter groups, including the Levellers, the Grundies and the Frontists, each with their own unique take on God's intended foundation garments.

Meanwhile, Cavalier underwear grew ever more extravagant, culminating in the infamous 'Marquess of Chippenham's Fancy'. Rumours that King Charles himself was wearing these dangerous fripperies added fuel to the tensions that inevitably erupted into Civil War and brought about a tragic cessation in underpant development. By the time of the Great Plague and the Great Fire, the nation's pants were in a total state, and the nation-state was total pants. The Restoration patched things up a bit, and fortunately better times were just around the bend.

Edmond Halley baits Newton with his Cox's Pippin following a heated session at Carlton House Terrace around 1685.

AGE OF ENLIGHTENMENT

1670

The late 1600s saw unprecedented advances in pant technology. Members of London's Royal Society (also known as the Invisible College because their early meetings, held without Cromwell's permission, were so secretive that no one turned up) made discoveries that laid the foundations of modern underwear. Today we are not only standing on the shoulders of these giants, we often find ourselves sitting in their comfortable underwear too.

Christopher Wren, for example, perfected the unsupported dome and the cantilever, though it took later innovators to combine the two in the Wonderbra. Robert Hooke experimented with samples of rubber freshly arrived from Brazil and revealed the laws of elasticity. Most significant of all, Isaac Newton took time off between inventing gravity and inhaling noxious alchemical brews to outline his laws of underwear in his groundbreaking work, the *Principia Fundamenta*. A notoriously prickly man, Newton fell out with almost everybody he ever met – a fact which may have inspired him to invent the union suit.

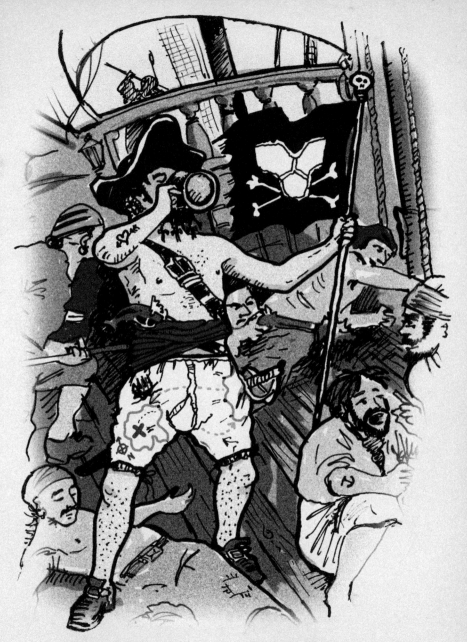

"Damn you all!", snorted Yellowpants as he downed another large flagon of Rum, "If ye wants a look at my smalls ye'll have to hang my bones first ye filthy sons of a deck swab!"

YELLOWPANTS

1730

In the early 18th century, pirates prowled the Caribbean making a complete mischief of themselves in search of treasure, adventure and accordions. Among the most diabolical was Yellowpants, worse by far even than Pantbeard, Long John Silver or the crew of the *Hairy Nun*. Yellowpants' plunder was vast and, like many a pirate, he buried his treasure on remote islands and relied on maps to retrieve it at a later date. Uniquely, Yellowpants turned his maps into a pair of primitive breeches so that he could keep them close to his person and avoid untrustworthy shipmates getting their rough hands on his jewels.

In time, however, the pirate diet and a series of spectacular tropical diseases caused an unavoidable deterioration in cartographic accuracy. So much so, in fact, that by the time Yellowpants was finally cornered and killed by HMS *Naughty* in 1730, the resulting mess of arrows, blobs and unidentified stains proved illegible to a frustrated Captain Dennis Hornblower. Undeterred, treasure hunters with a strong stomach still rummage through Yellowpants' underwear today, digging pointless holes from the Windward Islands to Swansea town centre in search of his fabulous booty.

REVOLUTION!

1789

Radical thought and a simmering resentment towards the ruling nobs, widely shared across Europe, finally boiled over in France in 1789. Of course, things had been close to revolting for some time, especially in restaurant toilets. The lavish attire of Louis XVI and his trophy wife Marie Antoinette enraged a starving population who were reguarly forced to eat the underpants of door-to-door salesmen simply in order to survive.

Unsurprisingly, the mob rioted and, in no time, the King and his wife found themselves in the Bastille awaiting revolutionary justice. History records that, as King Louis boarded the tumbril to the Place de la Révolution, the simple folk of Paris were struck dumb at the sight of his magnificent pantaloons. After the execution, these spectacular examples of the lingeriste's art had to be melted down and sold on the international market to prevent them becoming a counter-revolutionary rallying point.

Marie Antoinette insisted on being guillotined in her last remaining chemise, and is reputed to have been so silly that she was unaware she had been executed for some time afterwards. Believing the guillotine to be a new form of weight-loss treatment, she had to be shown a number of diagrams by Robespierre before finally passing away.

Back from Russia and not in the best of moods, Napoleon confronts the Chief Laundress at the Blanchisserie de la République. Despite the rumours, Madame Longuejean was probably no Russian agent, though she was certainly one of the most fanatical service washers in history. In 1805 she famously laundered the collected smalls of the Imperial Guard after the Battle of Austerlitz, a particularly nasty engagement followed by an equally savage deep wash with fifteen separate rinses and a five-day soak in bleach.

RAW IN EUROPE

1803–1815

As the dust settled from the Revolution, France's new ruler Napoleon Bonaparte seemed unstoppable, running amok all over Europe despite being the same height as a clothes dryer. With his foes at his feet he decided to turn east, and so it was that in 1812 an army of 500,000 imperial troops crossed into Mother Russia.

Sadly, due to a mix-up at the laundry there were barely enough pants for 200,000 men – and many of these were so severely starched that normal marching was virtually impossible. Those forced to go without saw the army's pride shrivel before them. The now-desperate French found all the laundries of Russia in flames, and at Sloggi on the Dnieper they discovered the charred remains of the imperial cotton mills, put to the torch to prevent the French from covering their rear. With winter upon them, the troops retreated home while Napoleon himself, convinced of treachery, came close to drowning in the Don basin.

The Duke of Wellington prided himself on the underwear he provided for his men. The rank and file were given the finest cotton smalls and were so grateful that they would have followed him anywhere, had it not been for the restraining order.

67

Hello sailor: Lady Hamilton welcomes Nelson back to Portsmouth at the end of another arduous campaign. This souvenir print proved highly popular with the patriotic British public, who have long held seamen in high regard.

THE FULL NELSON

1805

Lord Horatio Nelson, hero of many sea battles and generally dashing chap of action, conducted a scandalous affair with Emma Hamilton that set many tongues wagging in Regency England. Lady Hamilton, wife of the celebrated antiquarian thong collector Sir William, had a well-known weakness for quality smalls, and Nelson bombarded her with the finest lingerie money could buy. When his petty officer's cash ran out he resorted to intercepting French merchant vessels plying the lucrative 'Knickerbox' route through the Mediterranean.

Enraged French forces counter-attacked at the Battle of the Nile in 1798, but Nelson, desperate to gain favour with the beautiful Emma, routed the French and returned to his love with 17 captured brigs full of things for the weekend.

Alas, it was all for naught – following Nelson's untimely death at Trafalgar, Emma started a new life in Italy as a successful lingerie model, dying tragically at the age of 85 while attempting to fasten an oversprung corset.

Gambler, dandy and world authority on Rococo lace: Beau Brummel dressed up and looking like a thousand guineas in loose change.

DANDY DELUSIONS

1810

Flamboyance was all the rage in England by the 1790s, and hogging the limelight in centre stage was Beau Brummel, the greatest of all the dandies. Trained at the French *Academie D'ande* by some of the world's most fastidious popinjays, Brummel won gold at the Venice Festival of Foppery four years running, including a rare double award for freestyle promenading and pithy banter.

Brummel's underwear was outrageously expensive and, at times, completely out of control – he is reputed to have invented cross-dressing during a drunken card game with the Duke of Hove in 1808. But the hedonistic lifestyle took its toll and within a few years he was reduced to a penniless husk of a man. Finally, he succumbed to chronic verrucas in a Swindon poorhouse, and was buried in a pauper's grave and his last pair of Bavarian lambskin *unterhosen*.

Brummel inspired many to imitation, not least the Prince Regent himself. A short and styleless man, the Prince failed to cut a suitable dash, and had to be tutored extensively by Brummel and his ample manservant Dennis.

A CAST IRON BRIEF

1820

The industrial revolution brought many changes to the land, its people and its people's underwear drawers. So delighted were the people of Ironbridge with their new cast iron technology that they applied it to everything. After an abortive flirtation with cast iron hats, the Telford Iron Emporium previewed its first naughty metalwork at the Birmingham Fashion Week of 1821.

The benefits of the new cast iron collection lay, so its manufacturer claimed, in its ease of alteration. An uncomfortable cup size could easily be altered with a trip to the local blacksmith, and chafing or tearing would be relieved with a quick application of WD-40 to the affected area. Of course, the reality proved rather different, but for five long years, the women of Telford persisted in demonstrating the idea, hoping in vain to promote the technology despite their sagging figures.

Ironmaster's wife Florence Arkwright proudly prepares to batter her molten 32D 'Bullring' brassiere into a 42DD before a sceptical audience at the Wolverhampton Industrial Symposium of 1824.

BEATING AROUND
THE BUSH

1845

The discovery of Australia gave Britain a wonderful new place to dump its criminals, and the imposition of restrictive new underwear laws ensured high court judges had a regular supply of victims ready to pack off for penal correction. The courts targeted anyone they suspected of using underwear for less-than-proper purposes, such as fun, entertainment, or other moral impropriety, and as a result the stream of vessels heading for the Antipodes hosted some particularly risqué shipboard parties.

Dumped on the shore and told to find their own way to the nightclubs and bars of Sydney Harbour, many perished in the outback, victims of thirst, heatstroke and fallen arches. Backdoor spiders lay in wait for anyone seeking roadside relief. In time, however, these reluctant pioneers established Australia as an ideal destination for the tourist seeking alternative lifestyle experiences, while the motherland became increasingly suffocated by its own corset strings.

Pioneers on the road to Sydney included ancestors of Ned Kelly, Dame Edna Everage and Russell Crowe. Note the family resemblances.

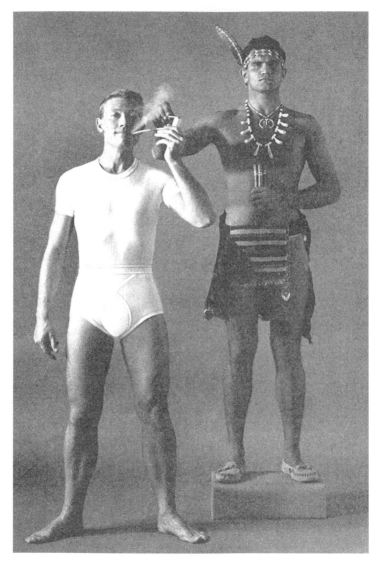

Dr Herbert Munsing proudly smokes the pipe of peace with a Balinese pant shaman. Darwin once said of Munsing that 'whereas some men think little of their underwear, Munsing's life was total pants'.

PANTS OF THE EMPIRE

1850

The mid-19th century saw the British Empire at its utmost. Scientists and collectors of the Empire ranged far and wide obtaining treasures to amuse Queen Victoria including plants, animals and native art. The British also sent collectors in search of all things underwear, of whom Dr Herbert Munsing was the most successful. Offering salt, beads and dressing gowns in exchange, Munsing managed to persuade whole swathes of South America, Africa and Asia to part with their undergarments, with no thought as to the eventual fall-out.

All through the 1850s Munsing sent consignments of underpants back to the Queen, who was forced to establish a special underpant closet in Kensington Palace, with a cubic capacity equal to Lake Windermere. Eventually, during an expedition to Oceania, Munsing pushed his luck too far in an ill-judged barter for the string vest and trunks of a tribal elder who had already purchased a kimono from a rival expedition. Facing death like a true Englishman, he was boilwashed in a giant casserole on the remote Pacific island of Le Creuset.

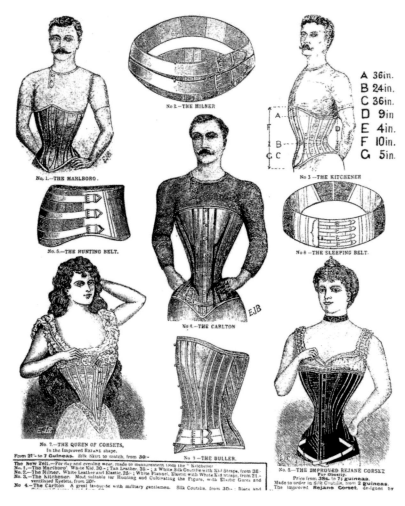

A 36in.
B 24in.
C 36in.
D 9in
E 4in.
F 10in.
G 5in.

No 2.—THE MILNER

No. 1.—THE MARLBORO.

No 3.—THE KITCHENER

No. 5.—THE HUNTING BELT.

No 6.—THE SLEEPING BELT.

No 4.—THE CARLTON

No. 7.—THE QUEEN OF CORSETS,
In the Improved REJANE shape.
From 2½- to 7 Guineas. Silk Skirt to match, from 30:-

No 9.—THE BULLER.

The New Zeit.—For day and evening wear, made to measurement from the " Kitchener."
No. 1.—The Marlboro'. White Kid, 30:- ; Tan Leather, 35:- ; A White Silk Coutille with Kid Straps, from 28:-
No. 2.—The Milner. White Leather and Elastic, 25:- ; White Flannel, Elastic with White Kid straps, from 21:-
No. 3.—The Kitchener. Most suitable for Hunting and Cultivating the Figure, with Elastic Gores and
ventilated Eyelets, from 30/-
No 4.—The Carlton. A great favourite with military gentlemen. Silk Coutile, from 30:- ; Black and

No. 8.—THE IMPROVED REJANE CORSET
For Obesity.
Price from 38s. to 7½ guineas.
Made to order in Silk Coutille, from 2 guineas.
The improved Rejane Corset, designed by

Corsets enjoyed great popularity in the Victorian era. So much so, in fact, that they were worn by men, women, children, cats, wasps and chairs. The result was a boom in the whaling industry, and a fad for long thin food that could pass through a severely compressed waistline. There was a price to pay, of course, and several people are known to have snapped in half or exploded during banquets.

THE GREAT EXHIBITIONIST

1851

The British Empire was now bigger and better than any previous empire and everyone was jolly pleased about it, unless they were foreign. In 1851 the Queen opened a huge festival in London in order to show the wonders of the Empire to the people of Britain, and the people from whom the wonders had been cunningly stolen only recently.

Keen to get in on the act was Lionel Slazenger, a one-time associate of Dr Crapper and inventor of the suspended steam corset. Despite guards posted on the doors of the Crystal Palace, Slazenger repeatedly managed to gain access and display his wares to the collected ambassadors and their children. Scandal ensued, and Slazenger was forced to move to Paris to escape both angry vigilantes and an affectionate security guard called Wallace Button.

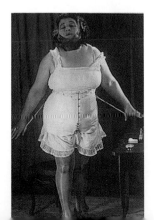

There was no denying the popularity of Slazenger's designs. Queen Victoria herself wore his spring-loaded 'Britannia' corset all through the Siege of Khartoum in a show of support for General Gordon.

WANTED

THE PANTYHOSE GANG

$5000 REWARD

**FOR ANY INFORMATION LEADING TO THE SUCCESSFUL ARREST
OF ALL OR ANY OF THE ABOVE OUTLAWS.
ISSUED BY THE WOMEN'S INSTITUTE, TUSCON BRANCH**

STICK 'EM UP!

1890

Legends of the Old West, the Pantyhose Gang ranged all over Arizona in a series of daring hold-ups. For five years they struck fear into the proprietors of lingerie boutiques from Tucson to Dead Man's Gusset. Clad only in the finest imported lace and silk, the gang soon had a price on their heads and the law finally decided that the time had come to bring the gang to justice.

Sheriff Herbert Hooper Jnr rode out with a posse of five hand-picked men in August 1890, but by October it was clear that they were not coming back. A second posse sent to find them also vanished. Over the following months, a dozen more posses set out in search of the girls' luxurious hideout, until finally the women of Tucson took matters into their own hands and, for the sake of their few remaining menfolk, confiscated their saddlebags and shot all their horses.

The Pantyhose Gang at the height of their notoriety – Jessie Aubade, The Floosie with No Name, Jade Gossard and Marie Jo.

Sheriff Kevin 'Mulebreath' McClusky prepares for the first posse of the spring. At one stage there was a five-month waiting list to go on the 'Pantyhose Trail'.

81

Watched by an understandably apprehensive
chamois, Balzac makes a final, desperate bid
for freedom in the mountains. Shepherds
in the high pastures claim that his spirit still
stalks the peaks. In 1995 a pair of perfectly
preserved boxer shorts were recovered from
the Bratwurst Glacier, though Balzac
himself was not inside them.

UP THE MATTERHORN

1908

Spurred on by Nietzsche's *Man and Superman,* the youth of Germany celebrated the new century by rejecting the *lederhosen* and, in wilful defiance of their elders, wearing their *unterhosen* outside their trousers. Going further, dedicated nudist and glockenspiel salesman Otto Von Balzac encouraged thousands of young Teutons to follow him into the Alps to hold a socks-and-pants music festival – *Das Birkenstock.* Headline act was Richard Wagner with his five-day laundry-based concept opera, the *Wring Cycle.* It was received ecstatically.

The difficult second opera, the *Spin Cycle,* stopped early due to a lack of coins. Pursued by angry fans, the escaping Balzac raced to the foot of the Matterhorn where he was last spotted rappelling purposefully up the mountain. Passing into the cloud base, the ardent naturist whipped off his makeshift *shortzpiel* and reached for his *Götterdämmerung.* Attempting to reassure his hysterical young wife, one pursuer cried: 'We can see your Balzac from here!' He was never seen again.

Emiline Pankhurst heads for a famous victory in the first Ladies' Invitational Penny Farthing Handicap at Chepstow, 1911. Seconds later, an outraged Edward VII leapt onto the course in only his union suit, suffering third-degree skidmarks in the ensuing chaos.

GIRL POWER

1910

As the invention of the liberty bodice in the 19th century finally allowed ladies to breathe more easily, the rush of oxygen to the brain meant they started to think about things that had previously been the concern of uncorseted men, including politics, trousers and bicycle outings.

Led by Emiline Pankhurst, the suffragette movement enraged Edwardian sense of values, but since most of these were second-hand Victorian values anyway, no one was terribly concerned. It was only when Pankhurst suggested that access to flexible underwear and voting rights might be extended to ladies' maids and other potential socialists that the trouble really began.

Socialist, feminist and literary icon Virginia Woolf relaxes at her typewriter in between drafts of Mrs Dalloway. *Despite her impeccable credentials and unreadable prose style, Woolf was secretly an underwear pioneer, shown here modelling the Wittingham two-stroke garter belt. She was also known to black up and cross-dress as an African boy in order to gain access to sailors.*

ASSAULT ON THE POLE

1912

By 1910, everyone who was anyone was heading off on foolhardy missions to plant flags at various poles. Hidden from respectable public gaze, the exotic dancers and performers of London's Mayfair were inspired by a works outing to the Royal Geographical Society to strike a blow for their trade and mount their own expedition. And so, in January 1912, after securing a sponsorship deal with Sir Ronald Damart, 15 girls from the Kit Kat Club set out from Port Raymond in a daring attempt to be the first erotic artistes on the pole.

As the expedition descended into a media circus, the establishment became uncomfortable. Ernest Shackleton was duly dispatched by the Navy to bring the women home, but became hopelessly lost after his sloop was trapped in pack ice. He and his crew were forced to sit out the winter on a remote island with only the ship's walrus for company. Meanwhile, the girls duly arrived at the pole and performed an artistic tableau for the huskies – the original 'pole dance'. Frostbite took its toll, however, and few returned to enjoy the fruits of their success.

Expedition leader Theodora Hempelman-Addams, with Titmus the dog, shows off her all-weather equipment to waiting photographers.

IF THIS CAN HAPPEN
in BELGIUM
WHATEVER NEXT?
CONVENT
BEAT THE HUNS AND SAVE THE NUNS
ENLIST

TRENCH PANT

1914

With everyone sick to death of peace and tranquility, a war was duly arranged by the Big Powers with lots of Small Powers invited whether they were interested or not. The beastly Germans kicked things off by marching around Belgium, stealing combinations, singlets and trunks from terrified civilians.

Most notorious were the 51st Bavarian Infantry Regiment, who were noted for wearing stolen undergarments on their spiked helmets during battle to intimidate the enemy. Outraged, the Allies hit back by sitting in muddy holes for four years, setting off whizz-bangs and emitting gas. Eventually this seemed to do the trick and the Kaiser and his army went back to Germany without any underpants at all.

Famous spy Mata Hari reads a coded message from the Kaiser, cunningly sent on the inside of a Selfridges 'Old Faithful' corset. Caught later with a map of the Western Front stitched into her bloomers, she was executed by firing squad.

The spirit of Archibald Henry Sternhouse prepares to drive Conan Doyle's two-litre Austin Gripper to Tunbridge Wells for a night of mayhem.

TABLE KNOCKERS

1920

As Europe recovered from war, a wave of spiritualist enthusiasm spread across the continent. Arthur Conan Doyle and his chums summoned the dead and encouraged them to bang on the table for the entertaiment of gathered luminaries, but they were to discover the unexpected consequences of meddling with the unknown. At one stage there was so much ectoplasm in Doyle's house that it inundated his underwear drawer and caused 17 pairs of his finest long johns to go on a two-day rampage around East Sussex.

One recently pressed union suit made it as far as the Forest of Dean before being hacked to bits by a startled woodman.

THE UNMENTIONABLES

1926

The U.S. prohibition of alcohol in the 1920s sparked a wave of crime in Chicago. Gangster warfare erupted in the eastside, upper southside, lower upside and near left upper downside, as rival mobs fought for control of the booze racket. Transporting the liquor was no easy matter, however, with tough cops willing to stand up for the law and intercept the shipments.

One solution was to use the fashionable 'bloomer', a panty with so much give that it could accommodate enough bottles of Old Ma Garter's Throatmelter Bourbon to keep a party popping for three days with only two liver washes. Crack detective Laurien O'Kite's team of Unmentionables were empowered with stop-and-search powers to stamp out bloomers, and it became compulsory to wear French knickers which, though capacious, had no elastic and hence no restraining pressure.

Seized by the Unmentionables on her way to a speakeasy, Mrs Capone is forced to unload her bloomers for the forensic department of the Chicago Police Department and their close friends.

The clothes maketh the policeman. Climate was no deterrent to the Unmentionables, who wore what in 1926 was the most advanced cold-weather union suit in existence. This page from an operational manual hints at its warming powers.

Buddy, can you spare a dime?
Desperate men fight for the last pair of boxers in the Dust Bowl.

HARD TIMES

1930

After it surged ahead during the roaring twenties, the ensuing slump of the depression left the global economy unable to get out of bed before lunch. Within days of the Wall Street Crash, billions had been wiped off the international smalls market and underpant workers now hung about, listless and unwanted. The unemployed soon learnt to make a single pair of button-fronted trunks satisfy a household of 15 for two years.

The fetish mills of Newcastle and Durham were particularly badly hit. In 1932 these proud men marched south to stalk the goverment, to the perturbation of everyone except the Lord Privy Seal. In America, Franklin Roosevelt's 'New Deal' encouraged a public underpant drive to get the boys back to work, while in Germany, Hitler created the *Volkshosen* or 'people's pant'. This was the start of a wide-ranging project to give his countrymen the freedom of movement he felt they deserved.

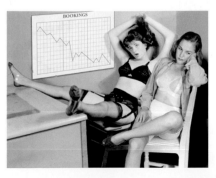

With no one buying, the once-huge lingerie market lay in lacy tatters. Many lingerie models, already weak from faddish diets, soon faded away and perished.

BRITAIN STANDS FIRM

A WORLD INFLAMED

1939

Keen to avenge the chronic underwear restrictions imposed under the Treaty of Versailles, Hitler stormed Poland and France, and by 1940 was poised to attack Great Britain. All that stood between defeat and survival were the Spitfires of the RAF and the British tradition of making sensible underpants that enabled pilots to fly and fight without chafing or embarrassing itching.

Goering, in contrast, ordered his pilots to fly in *lederhosen*. During combat these unwieldy smalls inhibited the Dorniers and crushed their ability to withstand the attacks of the RAF. Driven mad by pinching, the typical Messerschmitt pilot could barely withstand the heat of battle for a few minutes before fleeing back to base for debriefing and a talc rub-down.

With war raging, the British needed a stiff upper lip, amongst other things. Top peacetime underwear model turned fighter ace Simon 'Spanker' Watson helped raise the nation's spunk with this 1940 propaganda poster.

Leather flugwaffenunterhosen *such as these are widely believed to have cost the Luftwaffe the Battle of Britain. The fighters were worst affected — things were made easier for Heinkel bomber crews by the introduction in July 1940 of a laundry room and ironing board next to the bomb bay.*

TOP SECRET

From Brig. Gen. ...
SHAEF

17th May 1943

To HQ
Special Underwe...

RE: Training Op...

Sir,

I felt compelled ... ... role of observer during
the recent train... ... ly a great success and I am
sure all your pe... ... difficult months ahead.

I have just had ... ... w reminders of issues that
may come forth o... ... and these are listed below.

1. It will be likely that SUE agents will run into watery conditions on active service.
I suggest that the next training operation use water hoses to get the girls used to
the clinging effect of the underwear during rain or immersion in water such as
canals, rivers and warm soapy baths.

2. I have a catalogue of underpants from before the war that has some designs I think
might look or rather work well on the girls. In order to save strategic materials we
can use leather or latex in place of the rubber so popular now in occupied Holland.

3. If personnel are in short supply I am happy to hold the hoses needed for the water
simulation mentioned before.

4. I was wondering if you could supply officer only cubicles in time for the next
operation. The last splendid operation was only marred by an embarrassing altercation
with the Padre.

Yours sincerely

Brig. Gen. Earnest J. Minty DSO.

GOING COMMANDO

1942–44

With Europe lying trapped beneath the giant thigh-length boot of the Nazis, Churchill decided that the best way to hit back would be through secret agents inserted into occupied Europe. Many of these were plucky young women, rigorously trained to be ready for any eventuality. The Germans responded with their own elite force of dishy Fräuleins ready to combat British sabotage squads.

Wise to the British attachment to their standard-issue War Office smalls, the Gestapo were quick to frisk suspected agents for non-French underwear. As the problem became clear, the Army's elite underwear unit, based at Alton Towers, worked against the clock to kit out their brave spies in the most authentic underwear available. Despite this, the vital work of the Special Underwear Executive (SUE) went unrecognised until the 1950s and the release of the popular film *I Wore Monty's Y-fronts*.

Caught short only five miles from the Swiss border, Major St John Buffet DFC, TCP is cornered and uncovered by Nazi spymaster Otto Suggestion.

GÖTTERDÄMMERUNG

1945

By May 1945 it was clear that the Third Reich was unlikely to be invited back for a second series. In Berlin, Hitler's dreams of world domination lay limp and useless as all around him the German war machine folded under the Russian steam iron. In the bunker, the Führer brooded over a model of the proposed BMW *unterhosen* manufacturing plant, designed by Speer to replace the sprawling Regensburg Gusset Works blown to threads by the U.S. Eighth Airforce the year before. Now, to escape the retribution, all Nazi underwear was being buried deep underground.

With the Russians on the doorstep and with nothing clean to wear, Hitler became obsessed with avoiding capture without at least a change of socks. But it was not to be: after a last rummage through Goebbels' laundry basket, the tyrant shot himself, having drunk two tumblers of Vanish.

Eva Braun gets the bunker tidy for visitors, Berlin, May 1945. She is using the Me. H-500 Vundervac designed by Willy Messerschmitt, still rated as the most powerful vacuum ever used domestically, frequently removing trousers and hats from anyone within lethal radius. This example survived the war and its bag was recently opened live on the Discovery Channel. It was found to contain the mortal remains of Martin Bormann and a road map of Argentina.

Choosing between underwear or clothes became a constant dilemma. Here, my own dear grandmother, Edith Slapdancer of 15 Gasometer Terrace, Barnes, braves the crowds at a Coronation street party to make a celebratory cup of cha.

AUSTERITY PANTS

1949–53

With victory achieved, the British could sit back, relax and enjoy a period of abject misery and privation. Rationing, plus the dreary weather, put everyone in a right bloody mood and they all learnt to go without, not that they'd really had it in the first place of course.

Underwear was no exception. Due to shortages it was impossible to obtain decent toiletwear and soon the British learnt to queue for five days just to wear a pair of clean pants for half an hour before handing them back. On the black market there were smalls galore, if you had the cash, but for most, the idea of snow-white chest-high cotton Y-fronts remained the stuff of dreams. Only the Coronation could lift the gloom, and the whole Commonwealth tuned in to see Queen Elizabeth fitted with the Ermine Girdle of State.

Getting round the shortages became an obsession for many. Silk and nylon being in short supply, some took to making underwear from nettles.

*Elenya Ivanova Moss, the face of Soviet underwear for 20 years,
ponders an uncertain future in the Gulags.*

A RED WEDGE

1953

By the early 1950s, the Cold War had grown so chilly that even spies in three-ply woollen trunks were forced in from the cold for regular debriefing. One pivotal cause of tension was Stalin's sensitivity over the state of Soviet underwear. As early as 1945, Bess Truman and Mrs Attlee had been overheard making flippant remarks about communist corsetry on the sidelines of the Potsdam Conference, and a humiliated Stalin had immediately issued a Decree for the Modernisation of Soviet Underwear. As a first step, the cream of Russian pant design were rounded up and sent to the Urals. There, they would found a new, top-secret Design Bureau, OKB-362436.

By 1953 the team were ready to debut People's Patriotic Corset No. 8 at the Paris *Salon de Lingerie*. It proved a humiliating disaster, however, with several models suffering permanent whiplash. The collapse of Soviet underwear was a final blow to Stalin's failing health: one of his final decrees was to condemn the design team to forced labour in the Siberian elastic mines.

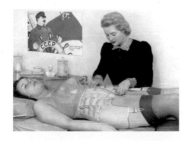

A labour-camp 'volunteer' is welded into People's Patriotic Corset No. 7.

UNDER THE BED

1955

The perceived threat of advanced Soviet underwear sparked a wave of paranoia in America. Senator Joseph McCarthy launched a crusade against anyone he suspected of being a communist, a liberal, or simply the kind of pinko who didn't keep their vest tucked securely into their underpants at all times.

Dire warnings of 'Reds under the bed' were taken literally by many anxious parents, to the embarrassment of their teenage sons. Large numbers of *National Geographic* magazines and Sears catalogues were recovered, but no communists. Desperate to keep his moral crusade going, McCarthy joined forces with FBI Director J. Edgar Hoover (a man said to have known a thing or two about corsets) to introduce on-the-spot fines for anyone caught wearing un-American underwear.

On college campus, some groups took pant inspection into their own hands. Popularly known as 'jocks' thanks to their own underwear habits, these athletic young men victimised those they perceived as suspiciously intelligent, which was just about everyone. Here, college baseball star 'Flash' Harrison enjoys beating a suspected nerd, while a young Donald Rumsfeld looks on.

TEENAGE KECKS

1961

As Beatlemania swept the globe it inspired a host of would-be Epsteins to try their hand in the pop world. One such hopeful was the infamous Barry Rump, who reasoned that the frenzy generated by the Beatles, Rolling Stones and Tommy Steele could be recreated fourfold if the performer was dressed in a clean set of skivvies.

The first of Rump's 'skivbeat' acts were the Fleshtones (aka Bendy, Philip, Twitch and Mackerel), the four-boy beat combo from Nuneaton still remembered for such hits as *Make me Proud, I'm Pointing the Way to San José* and *Nights in Bri Nylon*. Rump's other underwear-based acts included The Gussettes, Hugo Furst and the Graspers, and the Band of the West Midlands Police Force.

Girl power! The Gussettes in rehearsal: Blodwyn Jones (left) and Sheila Muffet.

The Fleshtones photographed at Dallas Airport at the start of their first U.S. tour. Bendy is wearing the all-in-one lilac union suit that caused such controversy in Idaho.

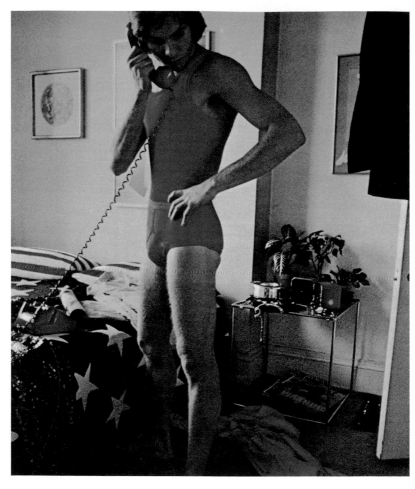

JFK takes a break from ironing to field a call from Russian premier and shoe fetishist Nikita Khrushchev at the height of the Cuban Missile Crisis.

CAMELOT

1961–1963

The inauguration of John F. Kennedy as U.S. President in 1961 gave new hope to America at a time when it was lagging behind in both the Space Race and the Under-War. JFK portrayed himself as young, dynamic and thrusting – a man not afraid to be photographed in his pants. The truth was rather different. When fully clothed, he endured constant pain from an ungainly surgical support. Nevertheless, this fiercely intelligent man steered America through some of its darkest hours, avoiding nuclear armageddon during the infamous Cuban Missile Crisis, when Fidel 'The Cigar' Castro tried to bring the latest Soviet corsetry within striking distance of the U.S. mainland by smuggling it inside innocent tactical nuclear weapons.

But the Kennedy dream ended all too soon on that fateful day in November 1963, when JFK was 'rubbed out' by the CIA for daring to suggest pulling U.S. troops out of Saigon's Pink Pussycat Club. Tragically for the future development of U.S. underwear, Kennedy was replaced by Lyndon B. Johnson, a man reputed to have worn the same combinations since 1937.

A young Lee Harvey Oswald pictured during a school visit to the Dallas Underpant Depository in 1947.

111

East German ambassador Maximillian Undspenser abandons plans for a walk home through Knightsbridge under the influence of Kim Philby's rum punch. Undspenser eventually defected to Saffron Walden, setting up a successful elastic wholesale business.

SPY GAMES

1966

Espionage reached epic levels in the 1960s. Double agents were particuarly fashionable and nowhere more so than in Cambridge, where spies were taught how to be unreliable, effete and communist as part of the national curriculum. The spies were divided into two camps (very camp and extremely camp), and preyed mercilessly on sexually repressed Eastern Bloc diplomats.

Since no one understands sexual repression more than the British, the embassy elite of the Warsaw Pact were soon feeling their effects. Even though these *agents provocateurs* twisted Bulgarian lingerie against itself at a number of saucy Belgravia parties, the results were disappointing. They learned little beyond the Russian word for 'thong' and the length of queues at the Kaliningrad branch of Naughty Cossack, the top Soviet transgender clothing retailer.

The KGB were not slow to identify the link between underwear and spying. Here Olga Legova, senior political officer at the Soviet embassy in London, poses for a private snap at a 1967 Court of St James reception.

Those who say nylon underwear is unfashionable, ugly and worrying should take a long hard look at this picture. For many, nylon brought a world of colour to the average citizen not seen since the Renaissance.

114

NYLON NIGHTMARES

1972

At first nylon seemed like such a good idea. Easy to make and available in a dazzling selection of colours and patterns, many rushed to embrace the new underwear. But no sooner had nylon smalls been widely adopted than the spectre of static electricity reared its ugly head. Lovers of underwear found themselves faced with a stark choice – dig out their traditional off-white cotton smalls, or revel in vivid pants that caused clocks to stop and attracted lightning. Inevitably, the public chose to stick with nylon and put up with the potential fall-out.

Soon, though, there were no working clocks in the whole of western Europe and it was not uncommon to return from a restaurant covered in spoons. Although OPEC pricing strategies eventually saw man-made fibres become prohibitively expensive (leading to the great underpant collapse of 1974), nylon briefs have recently been revived as a potential source of alternative power. Scientists have calculated that the static charge in a pair of leopard-print trunks is enough to power an iPod for 15 songs, so long as they are all by The Brotherhood of Man.

Revolutionary spirit spread far and wide. Here, women of Bolivia demand the right to wear thongs, something that had been strongly suppressed by the junta except on Friday nights. The CIA went to great lengths to eradicate radical underwear in South America, fearful of a domino effect whereby revealing G-strings could creep up on the American rear.

LIBERATION

1970–1975

Sick of male oppression and restrictive corsetry, in the 1970s women asserted their rights. Many questioned why men with beer bellies, Y-fronts and a barely adequate singlet were still insisting their womenfolk endure body-warping foundationwear with more moving parts than an Apollo spacecraft. The ritual burning of brassieres was widely recorded by the world's press, but less well known were the militant Corset Flamers of Islington.

Manufacturers were quick to respond, and as flame-retardant undergarmentry became common, the Flamers, keen to keep their movement going, took to burning socks, garter belts and, in a final act of defiance, *men's* underwear. Some extremists refused to let their patriarchal oppressors remove their trunks before stuffing them with firelighters. As a result, a few die-hard activists still reside in HM Prison Holloway, where they defiantly refuse to wear the regulation corrective teddy.

Initial solidarity among the Flamers soon turned to bitter factional in-fighting. Here, a member of the Dalston Women's Non-Nylon Liberation Committee (in white) slugs it out with the convenor of the League of Ladies' Post-Lace Revolutionary Army (in black).

Photo finish: Chester Whitlow of Great Britain powers ahead of Gunter Mule of Germany, Alex Rimshaft of Czechoslovakia and Frenchman Colin Sportiff at the 1983 Amsterdam Olympics.

GROIN STRAIN

1975

Sport and underpants have always walked hand in hand. Since sport was first invented there has been a need for secure, absorbent and stylish smalls that an athlete can wear with confidence in the most demanding of circumstances. It's a thin line between shorts and briefs, however, and underpant designers and spandex sportswear manufacturers argue endlessly about where one ends and the other begins.

Things came to a head at the 1975 European Athletic Championships when Jürgen Sinew of Denmark romped home in the 1,000 metres dressed in a camisole and lace string. Infuriated by the press attention for competitors wearing fetishwear in a range of track and field events, the authorities banned all underpants and bedroomwear from sport with immediate effect. This was rather unfair on judo and sumo wrestling, who'd been doing that kind of thing for years.

Weightlifter and sporting everyman Dennis Pilberry pumps it for the press just prior to testing positive for pile ointment at the Helsinki championships of 1987. Scandal followed, and fans saw the bottom fall out of sports sponsorship.

Summer holidays: open to a world of new possiblities, the young travelled like never before, keen to see even the most remote parts of the planet and ruin local economies by flashing their money belts. Here a group of gap-year underpant design students experience the authentic charm of ethnic cleansing on the Somalian frontline.

THE MODERN AGE

1990 – PRESENT DAY

As the new millennium approached, a rise in global awareness led the underpant elite to re-evaluate what was now a mainstay of the world economy. Mass communication brought once-obscure foreign pant ideas to the West: concerned pop stars turned the Aboriginal *gulangy* and even the formidable Inuit Kelp Pad into fashion accessories.

As global warming became a pressing issue, undergarments needed to justify their impact on the environment, and methane emissions weighed heavily in most people's minds. Many argued that it was senseless to fly underpants from the Peruvian rainforest to Great Britain when the tradition of making decent (though shapeless) trunks in the home counties was under increasing threat from EU gusset regulations. Meanwhile, despite global pressure, the US remained dominant, and the average American outstripped the rest of the world whenever possible. Global criticism of the US increased as President Bush exclaimed to an astonished United Nations that 'it's a perfect time for a Yank'.

New materials allowed designers to create sensational new underclothes for alternative lifestyles.

iPant

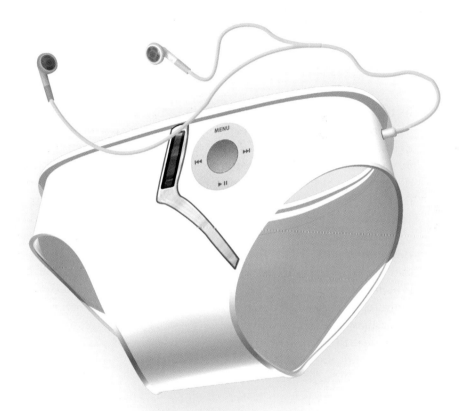

walk differently

Caution: may cause groinal shearing in some users. Remove before bathing.
To clean your iPant use only official iWash.

PANTS GO DIGITAL

2005

In the past few years underwear, like many other aspects of our lives, has entered the digital age. Early signs came with the launch of the Sinclair YF-81 and the AmStride in the early 1980s, but these were barely capable of simulating a game of Pong. It took the big guns of IBM and Apple to introduce the first user-friendly desktop pants in the 1990s, and consumers eventually got used to the idea of upgrading their pants every few years.

In the early 2000s Mr Jobs did it again with the iPant, but is there a dark side to these moulded plastic icons? With the addition of webcams, Bluetooth and wi-fi access, concerns are growing that we could soon see the first underwear viruses. Even more to the point, does our pants' ability to upload daily and even twice-daily blogs and report their status back to the manufacturer mean that Big Brother could soon be washing us?

In the old days, people used the telephone to tell each other the colour of their underwear. These days, our underwear can email pictures of itself to complete strangers without our permission — a time-saving innovation or an intrusion into our most private areas?

Living**Physics**

19 January 2008 No 1088345 WEEKLY £2.00 US $3.95

SUPERSTRINGS
LOOKING AT THE
UNDERPANTS OF GOD?

A TIMELY HISTORY
OF BRIEFS

2008

My suspicions of the connection between underpants and the fabric of the cosmos itself have recently been vindicated by the sensational work of maverick physicist and children's entertainer Marcus Hadron of Bucharest. Hadron offers the shocking hypothesis that the universe has the shape and consistency of a pair of ladies' smalls, and that these 'superstrings' exist in seven dimensions, one for every day of the week.

Furthermore, time travel is considered possible in this universe, with astronauts travelling through space and time via wormholes. This radical theory goes some way to explaining dark matter, a mysterious and annoying material that resists even the hottest of washes. Superstring theory also excites those of a more spiritual bent. They see an underpant-shaped universe as evidence of a benign female God who may have left us a message in the form of complex laundry instructions.

A seminal moment. Hadron's startling new theory is announced to the scientific community. Whilst some are only too willing to stand firmly behind Hadron, traditionalists complain that the concept has no meaningful support.

AFTERWORD

So here we must leave our rummage through the pants of time. I hope you have found the journey enlightening, and may now respect your smalls instead of laughing at them like a monkey.

But as we stand on the cusp of a new millennium, what do our skivvies hold for the future? Those of a mind similar to my own are looking long and hard, to prepare our briefs for the challenges ahead. Make no mistake, the future is uncertain, and underpants, like global warming, economic chaos and reality television, are an issue that, if badly handled, will ruin the land, devastate crops and make Saturday nights a complete wash-out. We are at a fork in the road, a seam in the gusset, and two legs, or rather paths, lie before us.

In one direction, we glimpse the sunlit uplands of a more enlightened society, where our unmentionables become mentionable, finally prominent in all aspects of daily life. Where we learn to respect our scanties and bestow upon them the dignity they so richly deserve.

In the other, we foresee a new brutal age where underwear is once again discarded and the rule of the jungle overwhelms the rule of the bottom drawer – for without our trunks we are untamed, savage and unpredictable.

For if, as recent developments seem to suggest, our underwear achieves sentience, then what will it think of those who mock it, soil it and accord it no status beyond that of a dishcloth? Will it not lash out at our arrogance, and remove us from it, as we have so often removed it from ourselves? Then we may find ourselves truly at the bottom of a laundry basket of our own making.

Time may be running out. I thank you.

FURTHER READING

The 2007 Report on Woven Elastic Narrow Fabrics for Underwear, Corsets, and Other Apparel: World Market Segmentation by City, **by Philip M. Parker**

Embroidering Underpants for Fun and Profit, **by Hazel McNoggin**

The 2007-2012 Outlook for Men's Underwear in Greater China, **by Philip M. Parker**

Trunks of Steel, **by Sven Hassel**

Twelve Years in a Yak-skin Mankini, **by Colonel Benjamin Lees**

Luftwaffe Unterhosen of the North Africa Campaign, Vol 2, **by Robert Forsyth**

The 2007-2012 Outlook for Women's Low-Rise Underwear in Greater China, **by Philip M. Parker**

Another Twelve Years in a Wire-wool Union Suit, **by Colonel Benjamin Lees (Mrs)**

The 2007-2012 World Outlook for Women's Control Underwear, **by Philip M. Parker**

Changing Times: Archaeology and Preservation of 17th Century Underwear, **by Dr Tanya Featherstone**

The 2007-2012 World Outlook for Women's Thong Underwear, **by Philip M. Parker**

Paxmanism: Understanding the New Philosophy of Pants, **by Nicholas Jenkins**

A Glowing Report: Underpants and Nuclear Submarine Safety, **by Stephen Finnigan**

The 2007-2012 World Outlook for Men's and Boy's Knit Underwear, Nightwear, and Robes Made from Purchased Fabrics, **by Philip M. Parker**

The Panticrucian Codex: Key to a Global Conspiracy, **by Giles Sparrow**

The 2007-2012 Outlook for Women's and Girl's Underwear, Slips, and Teddies Made from Purchased Fabrics Excluding Foundation Garments in Japan, **by Philip M. Parker**

Three Men in a Truss, **by Duncan Mallard**

The author would like to dedicate this bibliography to Philip M. Parker, without whom it would not have been possible.

PICTURE CREDITS